Light
Up The
Darkness

— (In God's Name) —

Michael Martin

ISBN 978-1-68517-743-0 (paperback)
ISBN 978-1-68517-744-7 (digital)

Christian Faith Publishing
832 Park Avenue
Meadville, PA 16335
www.christianfaithpublishing.com

Printed in the United States of America

Light up the Darkness

Light up the darkness in God's name!
Break generational curses so that they won't remain!

Become the difference that you want to see in someone else
If we are to change the world we must first start with ourselves

Let God guide you so that you may have sight
To illuminate the darkness in someone else's Life

Be the flame that ignites the fire!
Spread the love for others to aspire and reach higher!

Light up the darkness with God's love divine
Be a blessing to others and let your light shine!

Pay it forward to those in need
Illuminate the darkness and plant the seed!

Light up the Darkness in God's Name!
Shine light upon someone else's pain!

Let your warmth be a Blessing that heals a troubled soul
Let God bless you by helping others see their blessings unfold!

You are Beautiful and Unique

Learn to embrace the beauty within your God given vessel
Love who you are no matter your appearance because in God's
eyes you're special!

Regardless of Religion color creed or nationality
We were created exactly how God meant for us to be

True beauty is not in appearance but instead what's inside
Embrace the beauty within your soul and let it shine with pride

Each of us was born unique God's own work of art
Uniquely beautiful in our own way and unique within our hearts

Children of God and Royalty! That's what I see in the reflection
of you and me!
Instead of telling yourself that you can't become successful ask
yourself who are you not to be?

You are beautiful and then some! Whatever you aspire to do God
will help you become!

Once you set your mind to something and you start to believe
There's nothing in this world that God won't help you achieve

Let your heart aspire to keep reaching higher believing one day
you will succeed
Look into the mirror and choose faith over fear... Belief in God
and your reflection is all that you need!

A Daily Prayer

Dear Lord we humble our hearts to you on this day
We ask for your protection through these words that we pray!

To you we give the glory our almighty King
Please steer us clear from the evil that this day may bring

Give us wisdom and shine your light
When we are weak let us walk in faith and not by sight!

Let our spirit not be weary but instead be strong!
Guide our hearts to do what's right and deliver us from wrong!

Our father which art in heaven hallowed be thy name
Please comfort us in our times of fear and in our times of Pain!

Free our minds from worry in our times of doubt
Allow us to see Sunshine when we feel there's no way out!

Empower us with courage to make it through this day!
Dear Lord please hear us through these words that we pray!

Amen

May Peace Be With You

Strive to find peace in God and you'll find peace within yourself
Once you discover peace with God peace will come with everything else

Peace of mind is Golden and nobody can take it away
No matter the burden your mind is holding pray for peace throughout the day!

Rebuke worry fear insecurities and confusion
Don't let your mind become disillusioned

Don't let any demon diminish the light that you shine
Let your prayers allow you to embrace peace of mind!

Let your heart not be troubled and your worries be few
Reach out to God and he'll reach out to you

Life is too short so let your worries cease
Seek God for within him you'll find your peace

May peace be with you throughout each passing year
And may God's love reign supreme to take away your burdens and fears

A Family Prayer

Dear God please hear this prayer for I know that you are near
Please bless my family with love favor and joy throughout each
year

Please protect us with your grace and eliminate our fears
Allow us to become closer in our times of struggles and tears

Unite us with your strength and empower us with your love
When faced with dark days please shine your light from above

Dear God we humble ourselves and ask for your love divine
Please protect each family member and bring us closer through
time

Let us not be burdened with negativity and sorrows
Bless us with prosperity for each new tomorrow

Dear lord I Rebuke all demons in God's name
I ask you to bless our Sacred Domain!

Please bless our home for a beautiful life!
Dear God please hear this prayer and cast your light! Amen

Each day is a Blessing

Embrace happiness and give thanks for each day
Find joy in simple things and allow your heart to pray

Cherish each moment and try to find laughter
Tomorrow isn't promised nor is the day after

You only have one life to live so live it at your best
Learn to seize the good times and forget about the rest

Let your heart not be troubled because troubles will pass
Live each day like no tomorrow and as if it were your last

Learn to love yourself and try being Glad
Don't regret years later wishing that you had

Our time is precious and our days are few
Find happiness in Gods glory and in everything that you do

Each moment is a blessing don't let it slip away
Find strength in God's wisdom and give thanks for each day

A Nightly Prayer

Dear God I humbly ask within my heart
Please shine your light tonight while I rest peacefully in the dark

Please protect me with your Divine grace and allow no evil to enter my space

Dear God please hear this prayer for I know that you are near
Please let my spirit rest in peace and protect my Soul from fear!

Bless my dreams to be happy ones by shining your light
I humble my heart for you to give me Peace throughout this night

For you alone are Almighty in which I choose to abide
Please accept me in your kingdom and protect me by your side!

As I lay down tonight and fall asleep I pray dear Lord it's my soul that you keep
Please Rest my body safe and sound and if I shall pass may my soul become heaven bound

Please rebuke all evil that comes my way
Dear God I ask this in your name through these words that I Pray

Amen

Trust and Believe

In your times of worry and when questioned with doubt
With no end in sight and no way out

When you have prayed to the Lord time and again
And tried it your way but just can't win

When you have struggled trying to make it through another day
But the rain casts dark shadows that come your way

Trust in the Lord and let your heart believe
For there's nothing through his word that God cannot achieve

Anything in your heart can be fulfilled
If you rely on him and surrender your will

In life there will be many test's that we will face
But we must be encouraged and hold onto our faith

When you trust in God you are never alone
Your purpose is predestined and your seed already sewn

It's when we give up that our hopes and dreams will die
Only to later realize that we could've made it if we had only tried

Be Still

Sometimes it's best just to be still so that you'll be able to discover
what God wants you to feel
A Wisdom will come that you never before realized so remain still
and let God open your eyes

Let his voice guide you and your blessings will come
Stop trying to control what only God can and let his will be done

Be still silent and patient in your spirit
God often speaks in subtle voices when you open your heart to hear
it

Be humble wise and willing to listen
Rely only on God to make your decisions

Pray for guidance and surrender your will
Be calm slow down and for your own sake be still

Pray for clarity to relieve your mind and ask for God to send you
a sign

Embrace the Lords wisdom and to him be true
Don't let your own wisdom block Gods blessings for you

The next time that you make a decision it would behoove you
To silence your own voice and let Gods will move you

Continue to Rise

Take a moment to reflect on your life and what you've been through
Surely by now you must realize that God's been watching over you

When you felt hopeless with your spirit led astray and felt like giving up but instead you prayed anyway
Because deep in your heart you knew there was hope although difficult to cope with another day

At times when you didn't know how you would make it through
God still remained faithful shining his light on you

You may not be where you want to be and have further to go
But at least you're not where you used to be quite some time ago

Rise! Rise! And continue to Rise!
Let no weapon formed against you prosper or lead to your demise!

Hold your head up high through yet another day
Don't let your spirit become weakened or again become led astray

Your blessings will come that God has for you
Please don't give up regardless of what you're going through!

Continue to lift your hands towards the sky with hope and faith in your eyes
Knowing that the good Lord has brought you this far and that you'll continue to Rise!

Let God Heal You

With life comes smiles and also tears
Each shaping our character throughout the years

Hurt often teaches us the lessons that we learn
We get Disappointed, Upset, knocked down and burned

God will always allow your heart to heal
Lean not towards your own understanding but how he wants you
to feel

Your blessings are coming and they aren't far
Don't let your hurt change the Beauty of who you really are!

Heartaches come but don't let them last
Time heals all wounds and your pain will soon pass

Don't focus on the pain you're feeling instead pray to God for his
divine healing

Whatever you're going through it won't last much longer
Don't let it break your spirit but instead make you stronger!

Continue to pursue your dreams, aspirations, and endeavors
Knowing that God will heal your heartache and that soon you'll
feel better

A Pocket Filled with Faith

An empty pocket full of hope brings a heart full of faith
With little funds to help you cope your blessings still await

Appreciate what you already have even though you may want more
With a grateful heart there's no limit to what God has instore

Focus on your journey not your struggles in life
Embrace gratitude and God will bring your dreams to light

There's always someone else that's worse off than you
So always help with a couple of dollars even when you only have a few

Stay humble in prayer and money will come in time
No sense in worrying yourself so why burden your mind?

Money will never bring you true happiness in life
No matter how much we may desire we never get as much as we like

If you're faithful and patient you will make it through the long haul
And realize that with faith your pockets were never empty at all

When your funds are low and you're struggling in a ditch
Keep faith in God because with him you're already rich!

Life is A Gift

Life is short so treasure it as a gift
Pursue your endeavors and don't live life in what if

Seize each moment and love the life that you live
Never take life for granted or take more than you give

Life is a gift that you should behold so cherish each day that you're
still able to grow old
Let go of bad moments and take them in stride give praise for each
day that you're still alive

Our lives are precious and we only get one
So live it with no regrets for things you haven't done

Embrace each magical moment and find joy in simple things
Appreciate the beauty of life and the gift that it brings

Keep joy in your heart for our days here are few
Love others as you would have them love you

Cherish the gift that God has given to you
And Go after the dreams that you have yet to pursue

Honor your Elders

Honor your elders and let their life make you wise
Learn from their wisdom and let their lessons open your eyes

Seasons will change we learn and we grow
Sometimes uncertain what life will show

There will be highs and there will be lows
So learn from your elders wisdom because they already know

Honor your elders and be willing to learn
Let their knowledge make you wiser and become blessed in return

As they are now you'll one day be
Learn from their knowledge and let their lessons be your key

They've already done what you did and been where you're at
Their experience brings an abundance of wisdom that your life
may lack

Life brings uncertainty at the roll of a dice
So don't be reluctant to accept a wise Elders advice

You may think that you already know but may not be right
Their experience is Golden so listen to their life

Accept their wisdom and don't be stubborn or afraid
They only want you to learn from the mistakes that they made

You are not broken

Our trials and tribulations are a test of faith
God never gives us more than we can take

Don't get discouraged by your problems instead speak life
You are stronger than you think with the help of Jesus Christ

God can handle any problem that comes along
Through our will we are weak but through his will we are strong

Sometimes in life you will trip and stumble
But learn from life's lessons and try to stay humble

Let no weapon formed against you prosper or prevail!
Let no weapon formed against you allow you to fail!

You are not broken you are a child of the Lord
So stand tall and walk proud with your divine shield and sword

When your knees start to buckle let God carry the weight
In your darkest moments you may feel like bending but God won't
let you break

Forgive and Let go

Let he who is without sin cast the first stone
All too often we choose not to forgive and we forget the faults of
our own

No one was born perfect in this gift of life
And we all fall short from the glory of Jesus Christ

Forgive others and allow your peace to shine true
Don't burden your spirit by remembering acts that others have
done to you

We must learn to forgive if we are to grow
But we must first decide that we want to let go

When we let go our resentments will cease
Only then will we be able to find our own peace

If you have wronged someone then let them know
If someone has wronged you then forgive and let go

Sometimes others will insult disrespect and even offend
But forgive them with God's grace and allow your heart to mend

Focus on future blessings and leave your past behind
Free your heart and free your spirit from the burdens of your mind

Nobody is Perfect

You are not your past sins failures and mistakes
Don't let them hinder your life or the beauty that awaits

Everyone does things that they want to forget
And in our hearts we may sometimes hold regret

Remember that God has a forgiving heart so give God the glory
Keep in mind that your past doesn't dictate your whole life's story

Everyone carries mistakes that they have lived
Either as an adult or as a kid

Don't focus on things that can't be undone
Instead redeem yourself for better years to come

Repent for your past and leave it behind you
Don't give the devil satisfaction of letting your past bind you

Don't let your past stop you from being who God wants you to be
Let go of the past and let God's forgiveness set you free!

Baptism Day

No more walking in darkness after this special day I will walk in
the light and let God lead the way!
No more looking back on past sins I have done from this day
forward only new blessings will come!

As I'm riding to church with those thoughts on my mind
Ready to repent for my sins and leave them behind

I thought of all of the joy that awaits
My spirit filled with anticipation to walk in Gods faith

I arrived at my church and was led into a small room
With my pastor telling me that I will be baptized soon

I then approached the holy water without hesitation
My soul ready to be cleansed and my heart filled with anticipation

I lifted my hands into the air and closed my eyes
I then became immersed inside the holy water to be baptized

After I arose I felt years of pain cease
My soul filled with warmth and my spirit with peace

With my heart now cleansed and my soul redeemed
I'm able to see things that I have never before seen

I once was blind but now I can see
For the spirit of repentance has set me free

I once dwelled in darkness now I walk in the light
I am now reborn through the blood of Jesus Christ!

Amen

The Wise blind Man

There once was a blind man who long ago had sight
His eyes couldn't see but his spirit shined light

Long ago his sight had ceased but in his world of darkness he still
found his peace
With his words of wisdom he revealed to me that there is much
more to life than simply what we see

As I sat and talked with this wise blind man
I realized that he could see a lot more than I can

The more that we talked the more I began to realize
That I had been living my life through a pair of blind eyes

Blinded from the things that I should learn to treasure
Blinded from little things like life's simple pleasures

By talking to this man that had no one else
I couldn't help but take a deep look at myself

Things and people I took for granted in everyday life
This blind man treasured although he had no sight

He was poor in wealth although he was rich with peace
His appreciation for life didn't begin until his sight had ceased

And now this poem ends without furthermore
Just keep in mind that there's a lot to be grateful for

This wise blind man was happy and free
And made me realize that one doesn't need eyes to truly see!

After the Storm

Tough times will come but they won't remain
Continue to be strong and you shall make it through the rain

At times through the storm it may be difficult to see
But if you have faith you'll make it eventually

Keep hope in your heart and never lose your sight
For in the midst of darkness there will always be light

If your hope starts to fade in your times of doubt
Remember that it always rains the hardest right before the sun
comes out

You can and will make it through the storm just continue to be
strong
Tough times will come but they won't last for long

The rain will clear and the sun will shine
The worse will be over and pass in time

Hold onto that light that shines within you
It will bless you in the darkness and help guide you through

When the storm is finally over and the dark clouds have ceased
With your worries at rest and your mind at peace

You will then be able to turn back and look behind
Smiling and knowing that you've made it and that the sun has
shined!

The Devil is a liar

The devil takes no breaks and can come at any hour
So beware because he's tricky don't give into his power

He'll use anything or anyone to confuse your mind or weaken your
will
He's a deceptive liar that brings confusion so don't let him control
what you feel

Among his favorite things to use against us are friends and family
He uses the things and people we love most it's all a part of his
trickery

Temptation, money, drugs, and fear. He'll use anything to cloud
our minds from thinking clear

He wants us lost, hopeless, full of confusion despair and misery
He laughs while weaving his lies and illusions making you become
who he wants you to be

Rebuke his name for the Devil is a liar!
Rebuke his name and lift Gods name higher!

For greater is he who resides within me and protects me from
above
Through Christ I'm strengthened by his angels and empowered
with his love!

Choose your friends wisely

As sure as the sun shines another day
There will be good and bad spirits that come your way

Some people are truthful and some are deceiving
Some are divine and others bring demons

Some come with no purpose others come for a reason
Some come for a day others come for a season

Choose your company wisely don't let it choose you
Ask God to send only those friends that are true

Pay close attention to the company that you seek
For there will only be a few true friends that you should keep

Rid yourself of troubled spirits that are sad and bring tears
Treasure those that bring you joy throughout your years

Find those who have your best interest at heart
Learn to distinguish the good ones and bad ones apart

Choose those that brighten your spirit and make you laugh
And if you choose some but they don't choose you then they
weren't meant to have

What if God came Today?

What if God came today and you believed with all of your heart
That you thought you were ready only to be judged that you aren't?

Would you ask to be spared another day to repent for your sins to
be washed away?
Or would you bow and ask to be forgiven for the sins in life that
you once were living?

It is written that He will come and we will be judged for all that
we've done
Don't wait too long before you repent or wait till the day of
judgement

When the heavens descend and the judgement begins it will be
too late to repent for our sins

Prepare yourself for a better life and be ready for the second coming
of Jesus Christ
He is coming soon for there are many warning signs in this
confused world with uncertain times

Bow down and repent without hesitation to ensure eternal life and
your salvation
It's never too late to be forgiven for sins in your life and the way
you've been living

Let today be the day that your life starts anew
Be humble and be wise… Gods waiting for you

Let God guide you

In life there will be many roads that we will see
But without God there lies uncertain destiny

We must be careful of the road that we take
We must choose wisely for that path will determine our fate

Nobody can choose for us we must choose for ourselves
Only we have to walk it and nobody else

When it's all over said and done the path that you've chosen is the person you've become

Choose Gods path and have no regrets and as you follow his path may you truly be blessed
May it guide you to fulfill your destiny and allow true peace for you to be free

You'll never be blind to what may lie ahead if you follow Gods will in which you are led

The road that you take is what you will be
You can choose to be blind or let God's truth set you free

May you learn to embrace God and walk in his faith
He'll never steer you wrong nor will you ever have to fear what awaits

Don't create your own Demons

Think good thoughts and your blessings will come in time
True peace comes from within God and inside your mind

Don't create your own demons by your thoughts or actions
The devil is a liar so don't give him satisfaction

Don't let the devil weaken your will
Don't give him domain over what you think or feel

Rebuke the devils demons and break the curse
Negative thoughts only bring negative actions that will make life much worse

Rebuke all demons that try to enter your space
And Invoke Gods angels to take their place

Satan comes to steal rob and destroy any happiness that you may try to enjoy
Be wise to his ways for they are deceiving instead embrace Gods Glory and keep believing

Whatever we think our life will create and whatever we do determines our fate

Speak life and God will set you free
Speak life and break the chains of all negativity

Trust God and stay out of your own way
Empower yourself with the words that you pray

Embrace Gods Angels that bring blessings divine
Illuminate God's grace and let His light Shine!

Addiction

I can be the best friend that you ever had and also the worse that you'll ever know
I can pick you up when you're feeling sad only to return you to the darkest low

I can deceive you into believing that everything's well while all the time laughing as you cause your own hell
For my name is addiction and I have destroyed many lives by causing affliction and bringing demise

I can make life seem better and take away your pain by making you see sunshine when there is nothing but rain

In the end I will certainly drive you insane whether I be alcohol, marijuana, cigarettes or cocaine

I have robbed many of success and ambition, I'm your doctor, neighbor, lawyer and politician
I can temporarily take away your pain and fear only to cloud your mind from thinking clear

So the next time that you want to give into your temptations think twice and run for your life without hesitation

For my name is addiction and remember it well
Don't waste your life in misery by creating your own hell

Let go and Let God

My spirit grew tired of living in sin and not doing what was right
I kept falling short and lost faith in changing my life

I was scared because I didn't know what was instore
I was so far down and didn't know what to reach for

Many of days I would often ask God what his plan was for me
I was relying on myself but wasn't wise enough to see

I wondered why my world had become so broken and torn
I then asked for God's forgiveness and I became reborn

I now embrace Gods love and the gift that it holds
I humbled my heart and God saved my soul

Pray to God and let him be your friend
Don't block your blessings by not letting him in

Be blessed in Gods blood and start a new
Let Go and let God... He's waiting on you

Negative people

Rest for sure there will be those that talk behind your back
Because they don't have what you do or want to be where you're at

Without trying to get to know you they'll past judgment anyway
Or spread gossip and negativity for others to say

Quick to think they know you but really blind to see
They paint a picture of you in their mind based off their own envy

They are struggling with their own demons and fighting against themselves
They despise seeing joy and resent the happiness of someone else

Pay them no mind and ignore their views
People will often see what they want and think as they choose

Keep in mind that nothing beats a failure but a try
Remember that an eagle must first grow wings before it learns to fly

Success brings people that say you can't do it
Because they themselves are afraid to go through it

There will be those that are eager to doubt you
Also those who will talk about you

Continue to aspire and live your best life's story
In the end you'll be blessed and walking in glory

I Dreamed of Heaven

As I lay in silence with the nights quiet calm air
My eyes towards the sky after saying my prayers

I captured nature's beauty with the stars shining bright
I rested peacefully and in solace on this transcendent night

My thoughts in meditation surrounded around God's beautiful
creation
I drempt that I was in heaven with peace and salvation

In this dream that I had I felt God's grace
Illuminating the nighttime and blessing my space

Everyone in heaven was happy and free, at peace with Gods glory
living happily
There was beauty that one could not imagine to see and everyone
there was family

Smiling hearts, happy faces and peace beyond compare
Gods light shined on everyone with warmth in the air

As I dreamed on through the night in this divine dream
With my mind amazed from such beauty I've never seen

I began to feel the sunlight upon my face and had awakened to
another day in wonder and grace

I opened my eyes and wondered where I was at, then I closed them
again wishing that I could go back

But the sun had already rose to bring forth another day with its brilliant warmth and wonderful array

I hope one day to dream of heaven again where the angels will welcome me while I'm waiting to get in

But until that night comes I will patiently wait until I'm blessed once again to see heaven's gate.

God hears your Prayers

We pray for guidance in times of troubles and when the road ahead
is rough
We wonder how we'll make it through and sometimes if our
prayers are enough

One step forward two steps back its hard to smile when you want to
cry
When you hope for the best but get shot down it makes you not
even want to try

The lord hears your prayers and listens to every word
Especially the prayers that you think he hasn't heard

We often block our blessings by losing hope in the glory that awaits
God is there for you and he'll see you through so don't ever doubt
your faith

Keep praying to God and keep your faith your prayers aren't in
vain
He knows your trials and tribulations and also feels your pain

Let God reveal the answers and stop wondering what to do
All the while you've been praying to God and God's been listening
to you

He listens when nobody else has the time
He already knows your heart and what troubles your mind

God hears your prayers they don't fall on deaf ears
Let him relieve your worries and wipe away your tears

He's a listening ear that never goes away
He hears you when you talk to him and will always answer when you pray

They are our Future

Let them know that they're a blessing
Try to make sure that they learn from life's lessons

Make time to be your child's best friend
Love them unconditionally and with gentle discipline

Pick them up when they're feeling sad
Be the parent to them that you wish that you had

One day they will remember the things that you did
And that will be an example for them to raise their own kids

Listen to them and go that extra mile
Let them remind you of yourself when you were a child

Make time to listen and take time to care
So that they won't be lost and seek love from elsewhere

Teach them to trust in God above all else
And In time God will teach them to love themselves

Guide their hearts to God and let him light their flame
To break generational curses in his holy name

All that we can do is try our best
And it's up to God to handle the rest

About the Author

In this book Michael shares his testimony as a Christian that has experienced various obstacles in his life. As a disabled war veteran he realizes that life is a gift not to be taken for granted but appreciated even through troubled times.

Michael started writing and performing spiritual poetry as a teenager and also attended local open mic venues as a means of encouraging himself and others. As an adult he began making personalized gift cards and reciting spiritual poetry for various church organizations within the DC, Maryland and Virginia vicinity.

He has established himself as a spoken word poet by sharing his own experiences, strengths, and hope so that others may be empowered and receive enlightenment through Gods will.

Michael's aspirations for literary writing are to encourage, inspire, and humble the reader's heart, by sharing his testimony and offering hope from his own trials and tribulations.

CPSIA information can be obtained
at www.ICGtesting.com
Printed in the USA
BVHW031830120422
634093BV00010B/76